THE SPIRIT OF RESILIENCE

Recovering From Adversity in a Quick and Smooth Manner

By

Dr. Bridget Newton

Copyright © 2019 Dr. Bridget Newton

All rights reserved. This book or any portion thereof may not be reproduced or used in any manner whatsoever without the express written permission of the publisher except for the use of brief quotations in a book review. All scripture quotations are taken from the Holy Bible, King James Version & Ne-09744w International Version.

Printed in the United States of America

NEW Publishing Co.
P.O. Box 2461
Greenville, NC 27836

www.drbnewton.org

DEDICATION

This book is dedicated to my spiritual father in the gospel, the late Apostle Paul Thomas, who through the years have both taught and shown me the true meaning of what it means to be *resilient* and how not to die in my storm.

I had the privilege of watching him whether many storms but managed to survive the wind and the waves. Even when the tides were high and the winds were blowing tumultuously, somehow, he managed to keep his head above the water and continued to swim even though he was swimming on broken pieces!

Despite all he had to endure, sickness, pain, and the loss of his daughter just to name a few; he refused to give up or give in but instead he kept bouncing back and continued to fight. His life and legacy will forever resonate the true meaning and power of resiliency.

This book is also dedicated to those who find themselves shaken and shattered by the storms of life. May this book encourage you to know, that regardless of what you are facing right now, you will recover, because the spirit of resilience that resides in you has given you the ability to bounce back from the adverse and contrary winds that may be blowing in your life at this moment. Therefore; you will outlive your storm.

ACKNOWLEDGMENTS

Special thanks to my family and friends for your continued support. To Bishop Claudie and Delores Wilkins, whom I also esteem as my spiritual parents in the gospel. You have really shown me what it really means to have someone believe in you and always be in your corner. Your moral and financial support down through the years has helped me achieve many milestones in the Kingdom.

Thank you for seeing God in me and for seeing my heart as it relates to advancing the Kingdom of God. I can never repay you for the love and support you have given to me. Also, a special thanks to all my colleagues in the gospel for your encouragement and motivation.

FOREWORD

This inspiring book is a must read for any person that is facing adversity. Dr. Newton will motivate you to look at your struggles in a positive light. The words printed on these pages will usher you into the presence of the Lord and you will feel the spirit of resilience wake up and rise up in you. This book empowers the reader to embrace their struggles rather than despise and curse their adversities. Dr. Newton reminds us that God not only equipped us from birth, but built us to endure every one of life's challenges that we must face. As you read the pages in this book, an overcomer's anointing will fall fresh upon you, and you will undoubtedly realize that you possess the power within you to bounce back from anything that the enemy throws your way.

Dr. Pamela Holley

Table of Contents

Dedication i

Acknowledgements iii

Foreword v

Chapter 1
Recovering From Adversity..1

Chapter 2
Built For This..7

Chapter 3
Speak Life to It 17

Chapter 4
Get Up off the Floor 25

Chapter 5
Spirit of Comeback..29

Chapter 6
Accept that it's Over 39

Chapter 7
Making it on Broken Pieces..45

Chapter One

RECOVERING FROM ADVERSITY

Are you facing tremendous trials and unexpected situations that seemed to have knocked you off your feet? You are left wondering if you will ever regain consciousness and recover from it. Nevertheless, deep within you is an extraordinary strength that will cause you to rise back up, and before you know it, you will have bounced back from your situation. This strength is called "Resilience." Webster Dictionary defines it as *"the capacity to recover quickly from difficulties and the ability to bounce back into shape."* Because of the spirit of Resilience within you, you no longer have to succumb to depression, sadness or hopelessness which weigh you down and disrupt your happiness. The spirit within you is capable of helping you bounce back and recover from the adversity and opposition that you are facing at this present time.

Prov. 24:10 says, "That in the day of adversity you faint, your strength is small." The word **"faint"** means *"to let go, or to become disheartened."* The word "adversity" in this text means *"a tight place or a place of trouble."* Solomon was saying if we become disheartened when we are in a tight place or a place of trouble, our strength is small. It is in our tight places that cause resilience to come forth. How would we possibly know we could withstand pressure if we were never put into some very tight and uncomfortable situations? How would we know that God could bring us out of our most difficult circumstances if he didn't allow us to experience as such? Remember, Resilience shines the brightest in the darkest places.

The Spirit of resilience within you will cause you to bounce back and recover from everything the enemy has sent your way. As I aforestated, the word resilience means *"recovering readily from adversity."* Webster Dictionary defines the word "ready" as *"prompt, pronto, and without difficulty."* Therefore, your situation will be short-lived, and your recovery process will be speedy. God is going to hasten to bring you out of your situation with a mighty hand.

I urge you that while the winds of adversity are blowing your way that you remain prayerful and filled with God's word. Prov. 24:5 states; *"that a man of knowledge increases strength."* The more your knowledge increases, the more your strength increases, which fortifiy and makes you capable of overcoming the enemy.

You Can Bounce Back

When Joseph was hated and persecuted by his brothers, he never allowed their actions to cause him to run in a corner and hide. Neither did he crumble up and die. Even when he was thrown in a pit; he survived. Throughout his entire life, he was met with one challenge after another, but still, he survived. His positive attitude kept him alive. Wherever Joseph landed, he always bounced back from it. When he was thrown into the pit, he bounced back. When he was sold into slavery, he bounced back. When he was tested in Potiphar's house, he continued to bounce back. When he was unjustly thrown into prison, once again, Joseph bounced back. All throughout Joseph's life, he bounced back and recovered from opposition in a quick and smooth manner.

Joseph would have never bounced back if he had carried around an attitude of defeat and self-pity. He would have gone through life feeling sorry for himself and blaming God and his brothers for what he had to endure. But instead, Joseph was resilient, and would not allow what Satan meant for evil to keep him from reaching his destination and acquiring his promotion.

When it comes to dealing with adversity, you have to possess a Joseph's mentality. This mentality is that of an overcomer that causes you to bounce back repeatedly from the attacks of the enemy. If Satan can get you to succumb to the circumstances around you instead of continuing to fight the good fight of faith, then he has already declared victory over your life.

Attitude determines Altitude

There is a song entitled "Still I Rise" by Yolanda Adams. In this song, it admonishes us to never give up and never give in regardless of what we may be facing at this moment. It urges us to stand even when we are facing challenges. It admonishes us not succumb to the pressures of life, even though we may be undergoing trial after trial. Because, if the truth be told, we are all facing life's challenges and feeling the pressures and the woes of our society, but we must not allow it to overwhelm us, or dictate our attitude.

As Christians, we are not governed by the world system, but a Kingdom that is not of this world. We are just sojourners passing through. Knowing this; we can cast off the spirit of fret and begin to rejoice because God has given us a promise that no weapon formed against us will prosper. Therefore; you must maintain a victorious attitude in the midst of your situation, because your attitude will determine whether you win or lose, and whether or not you rise up or remain defeated. Your attitude will always determine your altitude. You must tell yourself, you will not give up or give in, but you will win, for this is your winning season!

"Fret not thyself because of evildoers, neither be thou envious of the workers of iniquity" (Psalms 37:1).

"That's the way God clothes the grass in the field. Today it's alive, and tomorrow it's thrown into an incinerator. So how much more will he clothe you people who have so little faith?

Don't ever worry and say, 'What are we going to eat?' or 'What are we going to drink?' or 'What are we going to wear?' Everyone is concerned about these things, and your heavenly Father certainly knows you need all of them.

But first, be concerned about his kingdom and what has his approval. Then all these things will be provided for you" (Matt. 6:30-33).

The Spirit of Resilience

Chapter Two

BUILT FOR THIS

The tests and trials you are experiencing right now have been permitted by God to strengthen you, and bring glory to his name. The greater the potential and the assignment on your life, the greater the trials will be and the more consistent they will come at you. James warns the church not to be surprised by the fiery trials that will come to test them; neither be alarmed when the storms come consistently, but instead; rejoice because they have been made more than conquerors.

"Beloved, think it not strange concerning the fiery trials which are to try you, as though some strange thing happened unto you" (I Pet 4:12).

When Jesus instructed the disciples to go to the other side, he knew a storm would arise that would challenge their faith, but yet he sent them anyway. His purpose for sending them was so they would believe that He was both Provider and Protector; therefore; not only could he feed the five thousand with two fish and five loaves, but He also had the power to calm the storm. When they saw that the winds and the waves obeyed him, it caused their faith to increase.

Satan had permission to touch Job's family and his material possessions, but he was unauthorized to touch his life. It may seem like what you are facing is going to be your demise, but I assure you that God already knows your limit. He will not allow your trials to be your demise.

Apostle Paul was challenged with test after test from the time he said YES to Jesus. He was hit with one trial after another; not to mention his time spent in prison. He was stricken with blindness, afterward he recovered. He was rejected by his brethren, he was met with perils often, fasting often, attacked by a viper, forsaken, and betrayed by his closest friends.

Why would a man that loved God as Apostle Paul and who was totally committed to carrying out the work of the Lord have to endure such afflictions? Before the trials came, God already knew what he had instilled within Apostle Paul. He knew that none of these things would move him, but that he would remain steadfast through it all. Just like He knew what he had placed in Apostle Paul, He already knows what he has placed inside of you. God knows that what you are facing right now is not going to destroy you. You just have to be convinced that it won't.

No matter what you are going through and suffering for his name's sake, it will not defeat you. He will not allow you to be tempted above what you are able.

The opposition that Apostle Paul had to endure was already factored into his kingdom assignment. The perils, the punishments, the imprisonments, and the persecutions were all inclusive in his call. When Paul was bitten by the viper, caught in the storm, beaten and cast into prison, God knew that none of these things would separate him from the love that was established in his heart. Your assignment will never be without adversity, but it is inclusive of everything it takes to fortify and equip you to walk in your purpose.

Apostle Paul was built to handle all the woes that came against him because of the grace that was upon his life. This same grace empowered him to stand against every wile and scheme of the enemy. If you are facing diver's trials that seem to be coming at you continually, rejoice, because God has counted you worthy to suffer for the sake of Christ.

God has also given you the grace to stand against

every plan of the enemy. You will not die in your storm, but you will survive. There is a supernatural inner strength that lies within you, that only comes forth when you are faced with tests and trials. Because of this, you can look at your trials and declare to them "You have been built for this."

What you have had to endure down through the years and in times past have only prepared and fortified you for this moment. So, no matter what the enemy brings your way, you can rejoice and count it all joy because nothing he sends will be able to immobilize, hinder, or keep you from stepping into the place God has ordained for you in this hour. God has made you target proof and the gates of hell will not prevail against you!

There is a toy called the *"Weeble Wobble"*– this toy has been designed to endure extreme pressure and withstand a great amount of force. Built within it is an inside mechanism that causes it to bounce back regardless of how hard it's hit. The harder it's hit, the more forcibly it bounces back. Just like the Weeble Wobble, "Resilience" is your inside mechanism. It will cause you to bounce back no matter how hard the blows you encounter. No matter what pressure comes against you, you will withstand it.

You are tougher than you think

As aforestated, there is an inner strength that resides within you that God has put there to help you get through the tough times in your life. He will not allow you to encounter anything that you have not been equipped to handle. Job said, "The Lord knoweth the way that I take." God knows everything about you. He knows what you can and cannot handle. God will never orchestrate a defeat in your life. Your trials are already on the losing end. You know the old saying goes *"Tough times don't last, but Tough people do."* You are tougher than you realize.

The late Whitney Houston sang a song entitled *"I Didn't Know My Own Strength."* In this song, she talked about how she had lost sight of her dreams because of the storms she was facing; Whitney had begun to lose hope until she realized that what she was going through was not meant to destroy her but to fortify her. Are you underestimating your strength? Are you allowing your tests and trials to predict your future? Allowing your sufferings to intimidate and paralyze you from moving forward only hinders you from reaching your destination.

As long as you see yourself as a victim, you will continue to carry around a victim's mentality, and therefore, the enemy will keep you on the floor waddling in self-pity.

But once you recognize what's on the inside of you and that you have the power within you to RISE again, you can pick yourself back up. You will see that all is not lost; therefore, you can once again reclaim your life and your dreams. Right in the midst of your storm; see yourself coming out on the other side.

When Whitney finally came through her storm, she realized that she had underestimated her strength. Right now, you are unsure of your strength. You are not convinced of what lies within you. You have to tell your circumstances that you were not built to crumble. It did not come to stay. But what you are facing right now has an expiration date. It does not matter how great the pain. You can't die in your situation when God has spoken life over you. God has declared in his word "you will not die but live to declare the works of the Lord."

Unless God allows you to go through some things, you will never know what you are truly made of. It is tough times that shape your character and bring out the best of who you are. They do not come into your life to make you fearful and defeat you, but to help you to rise to a new level of strength and power in the Almighty God that lives within you.

There have been many things that I have had to endure in my personal life, that if anyone had told me that I would have made it through, I would have never believed them. It was because I wasn't acquainted with my own strength. I could not see past what I was going through or the pain I was feeling at that moment. The tests and trials seemed like they were permanent fixtures in my life. I found it difficult to exhale because of the intensity of the pressure I was under. Many times, I didn't know if my afflictions would be my demise.

My tears became liquid prayers, both day and night. But there was something deep inside of me that continued to fight and refused to give up and give in. If you can muster up enough courage and hope in the midst of what you are going through right now, your life will begin to experience a turnaround right where you are. For your destiny is achieved through your perseverance. Even though there were times when I thought the situation would get the best of me, instead, I found myself becoming stronger and stronger each day. Till one day, I was totally delivered out of my situation.

After I had come through the storm, I found myself recollecting on what I had come through. I realized that while I was in the heat of the battle and allowing my tests and trials to talk to me, that I was permitting them to forecast my future. I did not recognize that I had underestimated my strength, and had almost given up on my future.

You will never know what you are capable of, or what lies within you until God allows you to be put to the test. Tests and trials are your friends even though they appear to be your enemies. They are there to help bring out the best in you and to help define and refine you so that you can become the man and woman God has chosen you to be.

Your tests and trials have a purpose that must be carried out in your life. That purpose must not be hindered but must fulfill what it has been commissioned to do. Your response to it should be, *"Have your way."* Allow it to do its perfect work in you so that when you come out, you will come out fully equipped and lacking nothing.

Today, you are much stronger and tougher than you think. One thing I have learned through my struggles and that is to have repeated victories in your life; you must learn how to outlast your storms. I am not trying to make light of your pain, but what I am trying to tell you is, that storms don't last; therefore, you will bounce back.

A Champion's Attitude

Staying down says you are defeated, but bouncing back declares you a winner. We are all hit with adversities in life, but we have to be determined to hit back just as hard. How do we hit back? We hit back with a champion's attitude. When a champion enters into the ring, he knows there is an enormous possibility that he can be severely injured, but because he recognizes his ability to defeat his opponent, he takes him on with a winner's attitude. Even though the blows coming at him are severe, he does not allow himself to roll over and die, but he fights to the very finish. This is what you have to do, you can't faint in the midst of the battle, but you must maintain a spirit and attitude of a champion and fight till the fight is over. You have already been declared the winner; but you have to keep fighting till the only one left standing is you.

Another way to fight back is through the spirit of praise. It does not matter how dark the situation may appear right now, give God the praise for bringing you through this. David said in Psalms 34:1 *"I will bless the Lord at all times; his praises shall continually be in my mouth."* David was declaring that regardless of what he was facing at that particular moment that praise would forever be on his lips. He did not just resign to praising

God when things were going well. He did not resign to praising God when things were going in his favor, and when things felt good. Instead, he made a conscious decision to praise God at all times, under any and every circumstance. When you begin to fight back like this, the enemy is put to flight. The enemy can't dwell in a praise atmosphere. Praise is your weapon in your season of adversity; so use it to counterattack the enemy.

Believe In Yourself

You can only achieve in life what you believe you can. Without believing in your ability to achieve is like driving a car without gas. No one has ever achieved anything that they did not believe they were capable of doing so. It doesn't matter how long you have been down or been in your present condition; you still have what it takes to bounce back. Tell your situation that it is not over until God has declared that it's over. Your faith and your ability to rise up out of your situation will be evident that there are no limits on what you can do when you put your mind to it and believe in the power of resurrection.

Chapter Three

SPEAK LIFE TO IT

Create an Atmosphere

Proverbs 18:21 says, "Life and death is in the power of the tongue." Therefore; we must be careful of the words that come forth out of our mouths during our times of testing. Words are powerful! They can create both positive and a negative atmosphere. If you do not guard your words, they can become a self-fulfilling prophecy in your life. If you are going to bounce back from your situation, you must watch how you use your words. Begin to speak positive and life-changing words to your situation. Romans 4:17-21 talks about Abraham being a man of faith, not considering his own body dead, unproductive, or lifeless but instead, against hope he believed in hope. He was fully persuaded that what God had promised him, he was well able to fulfill and also bring to pass what he had spoken. Abraham called those things which were not as though they were. This is the type of confession you must have when you are faced with what seems like a hopeless and dead situation.

David said in Psalms 23:4 "Yea, though I walk through the valley of the shadow of death, I will fear no evil, for thou art with me." David went through his valley experience with a positive attitude because he knew that, though he was in the valley, God was with him and was not going to leave him in that condition. Psalms16:10 says, "For thou wilt not leave my soul in hell; neither wilt thou suffer thine Holy One to see corruption."

David was fully persuaded that the valley was just a temporary location and that his location did not determine his destination. Where you are and what you are going through right now is not a reflection of where God is taking you. God is taking you to the mountain, but you have to first go through your valley experience before he brings you to it. As wonderful as it may feel to be on the mountain, the truth of the matter is we cannot remain there, we all have to pass through a valley experience in this life.

In Ezekiel 37: 1-14, God took Ezekiel to a valley of dry bones. The valley of dry bones represented a place of hopelessness and death. This may be where you find yourself right now. God raised the question to Ezekiel,

"Can these bones live?" His verbal response determined the future of whether the bones would come to life or remain as they were. The words of your mouth determine the outcome of your situation. I admonish you to speak life to it!

Prophesy to your Future

The dryness of these bones signified that life once existed. God asked Ezekiel if he believed that life could be restored back into the dry bones. Do you believe that life can come back to your seemingly dead situation? Do you believe that you can still rise again after all you have been through? Do you believe that there is a possibility of restoration? If so, you can live again!

Ezekiel, after he had assessed the situation, responded to God by saying, "Thou knowest." God had foreknowledge of the future state of the dry bones. I want you to know that no matter how dry and lifeless your situation looks right now, God already knows your future. Your present nor your past circumstances determine your tomorrow. Your future belongs to God, and he has promised in Jeremiah 29:11 that he would give you a hope and a bright future. Right where you are iis the perfect opportunity to give God praise!

God continued to instruct Ezekiel to prophesy to those dry and lifeless bones and command them to hear the word of the Lord. So, he did as God had instructed him, and as he prophesied, sinews and flesh begin to come on the bones. You have to prophesy to your situation and tell it to hear the Word of the Lord concerning your future. It does not matter how dim it looks right now; it doesn't matter how dry and hopeless you may be feeling at this time; prophesy life to it, and command your emotions to align with God's ordained plan and purpose for your life.

After the Word of the Lord was released over the bones; they still remained lifeless. How many times have the Word of the Lord been spoken over you and yet you continue to feel lifeless and hopeless? You prayed, fasted, isolated yourself, and have done a myriad of things to change your situation, trying whatever necessary to bring you out of it, but you still experience minimal victories. Maybe, the missing element needed to bring life to your dead situation is *"Ruach"* which is "the breath of God."

God spoke to Ezekiel again and told him to prophesy to the four winds and command breath to be released into the bones. The only thing the bones needed to be brought back to life was the Ruach. As soon as the breath was released into the nostrils of the dry bones, not only did they come alive, but they stood on their feet as a great army. When the breath of God enters your life, you will not only come alive but you will rise to a new position in your spirit, soul, and body.

While you are in your valley experience, you have to look past what you are seeing with your natural eyes, and believe what God has spoken concerning you will come to pass. Believe that you will live again after the pain, the storm, the rain, the rejection, the betrayal, and the losses you have suffered. Be willing to prophesy to your situation and your future. You will rise again as a great and mighty man/woman of God. Your future lies in your confession. So speak life to it!

After God had restored life back to the dry bones, Ezekiel was commanded to prophesy their future. The dry bones represented the nation of Israel. They had been in a state of dryness so long, they took on the spirit of hopelessness and felt that God had cast them away; therefore, they cast aside their confidence. Their present state looked like it would be the end of their reign in the earth. But God had another plan that would surpass their wildest imagination.

God's plan was to bring them out of their graves, place his spirit in them and return them to their predestined state. I want you to know God has a plan for your life that is bigger and greater than what you can think, or imagine. His plans are to prosper you and bring you to an expected end. Your situation has nothing to do with your destination.

God is interested in you rising again so that others can see the magnificence of his glory upon your life. This is why it is imperative that you do not die in the storm, but trust in what God has promised you and allow that to be the anchor in which you hold on to till God brings you up and out of your valley. Faithful is he that promised, who will also do it!

I know you have heard time and time again that your best is yet to come, It seems like a cliché, but I declare to you the Word of the Lord in this season of your life, and that is your best is yet to come, and that everything you have lost in your valley experience, God is going to restore it back to you. He's going to restore the years the cankerworm, palmerworm, and the locust hath eaten. He is going to compensate you for not giving up or giving in.

He is going to reward you far beyond what your mind can comprehend. Your future may look dark and gloomy right now, but it is getting ready to experience a turnaround. Your trial has an expiration date. God is going to clothe you and speak life back into you just like Ezekiel did to the dry bones. He's getting ready to resurrect you and make you a part of a mighty army that he is raising up in this hour.

The valley experiences that brought you tears and much pain has not been in vain; you have not lost anything. God already had your experiences calculated into his compensation plan reserved just for you. After you have gone through this experience, get ready to rejoice because you are next in line for a miracle. Your breakthrough is on the way!

"The hand of the Lord was upon me, and he brought me out in the Spirit of the Lord and set me down in the middle of the valley; it was full of bones. And he led me around among them, and behold, there were very many on the surface of the valley, and behold, they were very dry. And he said to me, "Son of man, can these bones live?" And I answered, "O Lord God, you know." Then he said to me, "Prophesy over these bones and say to them, O dry bones, hear the word of the Lord. Thus says the Lord God to these bones: Behold, I will cause breath to enter you, and you shall live. And I will lay sinews upon you and will cause flesh to come upon you, and cover you with skin, and put breath in you, and you shall live, and you shall know that I am the Lord."

So I prophesied as I was commanded. And as I prophesied,

there was a sound, and behold, a rattling, and the bones came together, bone to its bone. And I looked, and behold, there were sinews on them, and flesh had come upon them, and skin had covered them. But there was no breath in them. Then he said to me, "Prophesy to the breath; prophesy, son of man, and say to the breath, Thus says the Lord God: Come from the four winds, O breath, and breathe on these slain, that they may live." So I prophesied as he commanded me, and the breath came into them, and they lived and stood on their feet, an exceedingly great army.

Then he said to me, "Son of man, these bones are the whole house of Israel. Behold, they say, 'Our bones are dried up, and our hope is lost; we are indeed cut off." Therefore prophesy, and say to them, Thus says the Lord God: Behold, I will open your graves and raise you from your graves, O my people. And I will bring you into the land of Israel. And you shall know that I am the Lord, when I open your graves and raise you from your graves, O my people. And I will put my Spirit within you, and you shall live, and I will place you in your own land. Then you shall know that I am the Lord; I have spoken, and I will do it, declares the Lord (Ezek. 37:1-14).

Chapter Four

GET UP OFF THE FLOOR

You've Fallen, and You can Get UP

Donnie McClurkin sang a song entitled "We Fall Down." The lyrics speak about how a saint that falls and gets back up. In the song, the saint is not left in a defeated position. No matter what you are encountering at this moment, God will never leave you in a defeated position. David said in Psalms: 16:10, "Thou will not leave my soul in hell." You may have fallen, but you can get back up.

The problem is not falling; the problem is staying down. There is a commercial that says, "I've Fallen, and I can't get up." This, however, was a very unfortunate situation that happened to an elderly woman that had fallen. Because there was no one present to help her or anything within her reach to help pull her up, therefore; she had to endure the hardship of remaining on the floor.

The enemy wants you to adopt this same negative

declaration for your life. *Don't buy into it*! There is hope for the righteous; you do not have to remain on the floor. Proverbs 24:16 declares, though a righteous man fall seven times; he will rise back up. Before you are knocked down, he's right there to pick you up, because He is a present help in times of trouble. He has given you his Word to lean on and to pull yourself back up. What's keeping you down? Are you waiting for someone to pick you up?

Let Go of the Floor Mentality

You may have been hurt, abused, and rejected, and things may not be going your way, but you are not defeated. You don't have to walk around with your head hanging down, feeling depressed, and needing someone to pick you up. You are not a victim; the fact that you are still alive to tell your story makes you an overcomer. My concern is not you falling on the floor; my concern is you getting back up after you have fallen. The strength lies in the getting up. It takes no extraordinary strength to fall, but it does take extraordinary strength to get back up.

I know you feel as though your entire world has been shattered and you feel wounded deep within, but God will not leave you in a broken condition. He is going to bind up every wound. It may look like what you are facing, and the pain you are feeling will never go away, but I promise you, time will bring about a change. You have to keep moving and not allow yourself to become immobilized by your emotions and what you see. You are not the only one whose heart has been broken, and whose dreams have been shattered. There are many others that carry the same scars you carry and have felt the same pain you are feeling right now. You are not in this alone; you are compassed about with many cloud of witnesses. This is what you must believe and hold on to if you are going to get up off the floor.

You must see yourself not as you are at this present time, but as you will be. Call those things which are not as though they were. Call yourself healed. Call yourself restored. Your positive confession will cause you to rise back up! Your position can change, and you can experience wholeness in your present state. No more waddling on the floor, and throwing a pity party; you do not have the license or the permission to remain there. This is only temporary ground until you regain your stamina and pick yourself back up. As Yolanda Adams sings the lyrics in "Still I Rise"- *"Shattered but not broken, wounded but time will heal."* You must tell yourself you will heal from this situation.

Yes, you have fallen, but you can get back up!

The Spirit of Resilience

Chapter Five

THE SPIRIT OF COMEBACK

You Are the Main Player

In the movie arena, there are main players; because they have been labeled as such, their role is more viewed than the other cast. The producer has already written and predetermined the future of the main player. Even though they will encounter some very harsh and dangerous scenes, it is already pre-written in the script that they will not face death. The opponent or the opposition may bring them to a place of despair, but it is predestined that they will survive.

All truth is parallel, as it is in the natural, so it is in the spiritual. You have been declared the main player in your situation, and your outcome has already been determined. God has already factored in your victory in every one of your battles. But there are scenes of life that you must go through before you can get to your expected end. These scenes are called "adversity and opposition" they have been designed to break your spirit and cause you to abort your future. But because you are the main player, these scenes have been scripted in to work for you and not against you.

As the main player, you must understand that death is impossible, but survival is guaranteed. With that said you must not go into the battle with an attitude of defeat but that of a winner. Romans 8:37 states that we have been made more than a conqueror through Christ who loves us. This means we have already been declared winners before we enter the ring.

Learn To Encourage Yourself

While you are going through your toughest trials, you must learn how to encourage yourself in the Lord. Don't depend and rely on someone else to encourage you, or pat you on the back. You have to become your own benefactor in helping yourself come out of your dilemma. For there will be times that God will not allow people to speak into your life or be attainable for you to reach. This is so that you won't depend or ride on the encouragement of men.

God wants you to trust him with all your heart and lean not to your understanding. He wants you to believe in his supernatural ability to bring you out. He wants you to trust his ability to sustain and preserve you while you are in the fire.

When there is no one around to give you a word of inspiration and motivation, engage yourself in the Word of God, and allow the Word of the Lord to inspire and motivate you. The Word will speak to you in your darkest season. God knows what you are up against, and he knows that the enemy has come in and stolen from you. But don't allow what he has done to paralyze you with fear to the point that you continue to stay down and engage in a pity party. You cannot allow him to immobilize your pursuit to get back up and live again. You have to decide what recourse you are going to take to regain control of your life. David was not willing to sit idly by and allow the enemy to enjoy the pleasures of what God had given him. After seeing what happened; he knew he had to do something.

"And David was greatly distressed; for the people spake of stoning him, because the soul of all the people was grieved, every man for his sons and for his daughters: but David encouraged himself in the LORD his God" (1 Samuel 30:6).

It's Time to Seek the Lord

David did what the majority of us fail to do when we are in the heat of battle. He enquired of the Lord! It is important that we seek the Lord when we are faced with situations beyond our human ability to control. Jesus instructed us to seek him while he may be found, and call upon him while he is near. If ever we needed to seek the Lord, the time is now. James 1:5 says if any man lacks wisdom, let him ask of God. Anything you need from God, you can find it in his presence.

Jesus said we should always pray and not faint. He warned us to be careful for nothing, but in everything by prayer, make our request known to God. God invites us into his presence. The Word says in Psalm 16:11 "In the presence of the Lord is the fullness of joy." It is in God's presence that we receive the instructions and wisdom we need to handle any situation.

Staying in prayer fortifies you for every battle, obstacle, or adversity you may have to encounter. It is when we go in our own strength that we experience defeat. As long as the children of Israel had the Ark of the Covenant, which represented the presence of God in their camp, they won every battle. But as soon as the ark was taken away from them, they began to have repeated defeats.

The presence of God must take precedence over everything else in your life if you want to continue to live a life of victory. God must become your priority and your passion. You must begin to pursue him out of desire and not out of obligation. God has the solutions to your problems. He is just waiting for you to come in and sup with him. He's waiting to hear from you!

David enquired the counsel of the Lord as to what he should do in his situation and what recourse should be taken to get back their families and possessions. David wanted to know the heart of God on the matter. So he asked God, should he pursue his enemies? Not only did God give him a resounding yes, and instructed him to pursue, but he gave him a promise that he would overtake and recover all.

While you are under the attack of the enemy, you need the counsel of God with you. Because with God's counsel comes his protection and his promises. David and his men could go up against the enemy with confidence because they were assured that they were going to win the battle and recover all of their possessions. They were bound to score a major landslide against the enemy.

"And David inquired at the LORD, saying, Shall I pursue after this troop? Shall I overtake them? And he answered him,

Pursue: for thou shalt surely overtake them, and without fail recover all" (1 Samuel 30:8).

God does not only want you to retrieve your stuff, but he wants you to defeat and destroy the enemies that came up against you and stole your possessions. When David went into the enemy's camp to get his stuff, he left not one of his enemies standing. You can't afford to allow the enemies of your soul to live.

You are not fighting against flesh and blood but spiritual wickedness in high places. Satan is out to rob you of everything you own. His job is to kill, steal, and destroy. He does his job very well, so you must do yours even better. You must not allow him to carry out his agenda another day as it relates to subtracting from your life. Not only did David destroy his enemies, but he also recovered everything he lost and more. God is going to give you double for your trouble. Everything you lost and everything that has been taken from you, the enemy is going to have to give it back to you with interest. God is going to restore the years the cankerworm, the palmerworm, and the locust hath eaten. And without fail, you shall recover all!

"And I will restore to you the years that the locust, the cankerworm, and the caterpillar, and the palmerworm hath eaten" (Joel 2:25).

Pursue

As an overcomer; you must take on the Spirit of Pursuit. This means, you must be willing to go after and take back what the devil has stolen from you. The word pursue in the Webster Dictionary means to *"go after, to quest after, to follow-up."* Unless you are willing to pursue your stuff, you will not experience restoration or restitution. Therefore, to get something, you must be willing to do something. No one is going to bring your stuff to you on a silver platter. You must be willing to pick yourself up by the bootstraps and go get your stuff.

What if David had waited until the enemy brought back his stuff? He would have never received it, and the people would have stoned him. David understood the importance of pursuing. You must begin to understand the significance of it also. The time to pursue your deliverance, healing and victory is now.

When David and his men went in the enemy's territory and took back their stuff, not only did they retrieve their belongings, but they also confiscated everything the enemy possessed. This is because the Word of God has declared that once the enemy who stole from you is apprehended; He must restore back to you seven times over.

David and his men brought back a surplus from the enemy's camp so much so that they had enough to divide amongst all that were a part of his company, even those that were left behind due to the fatigue and stress of the battle. When God allows you to get your stuff back, he is going to make sure you come out with more than enough because he is El'Shaddai- the *"God of more than enough."* Everything that Satan stole from you will be restored with interest.

Recover

This is the hour and the day of recovery for all those that lost something in their night season. When you are allowed to recover something, you are given the opportunity and the privilege to regain and recuperate your losses. How many losses have we suffered in the body of Christ, in our families, in our homes, and in our communities? During this economy, people have suffered many losses, trying to stay on top and not be overcome by the pressures of bills, relationships, lack of money, loss of jobs, and etc.

I want you to know that recovery is inevitable for the believer, for those who have walked upright before the Lord and have honored him with the first fruit of their life. God is not going to allow your sacrifices to go unnoticed.

When David went into the enemy's camp, not only did he obtain his goods, but he obtained the enemy's belongings also. Because of David's tenacity, obedience to the Lord and his willingness to pursue his inheritance, God awarded him punitive damages to make up for the heartache, and the distress that the enemy caused him and his people. When you go to recover your possessions, God is going to make sure you are compensated for all you went through while your stuff was in the enemy's camp.

The Spirit of Resilience

Chapter Six

ACCEPT THAT IT'S OVER

Embracing a New Chapter

I have discovered that letting go is a problem that is so prevalent in the lives of those that have been rejected, abused or dealing with some kind of loss; mainly because of failing to recognize and accept when things have come to an end. In the religious world, the benediction always comes at the end of a service or an event. It is not until everything has been carried out that was pre-ordained that the benediction is given.

Everything has a starting and stopping point. Therefore; certain things in your life has to come to a close in order for you to step into a new venture. The use of a period in the English language means the end of a sentence or statement. It also symbolizes the end of a thought and the beginning of another. Right now, you are at a period in your life.

The people that were once a part of your life may

have carried out their assignment and purpose in your life, and it's now time for you to pronounce a benediction, so that you can move on to the next chapter God has purposed for you.

As aforestated, the moment you learn to accept that things are over is when you will truly begin to heal and bounce back from it. When there is a sense of hope still lurking in your mind, the desire and the determination to bounce back becomes more problematic, and the process is prolonged. Facing the grim reality that people and things have left your life, and understanding that they were only meant to be temporal will enable you to move forward, and cause you to see the situation not as an ending, but a beginning of a new season in your life.

Continuing to hold on to that which no longer has a pulse in your life will cause significant repercussions. These repercussions can impede your progress and prolong your recovery in bouncing back. Trust God to give you grace and strength to get through the pain. He will help you to make the necessary adjustments to make a quick and smooth transition.

When you begin to embrace and celebrate the periods in your life is when you will begin to move forward and embark on something new and fresh. Phil 3:13 says "I count not myself to have apprehended, but one thing I do forgetting those things that are behind, I press towards the mark of the high calling of God in Christ Jesus." Apostle Paul understood the significance of periods. To achieve what he was reaching for, he recognized he had to let go of the past. As I stated in my previous book, until you are willing to divorce your past you can't possibly marry your future.

The depression, sadness, despair, abuse, and pain of the past can only hold you captive and dominate your life if you allow it. You have to decide when you have been down long enough. After you have made this determination, the ability to rise back up already resides within you. You have the power to speak to your circumstance and tell it that it's over and that it no longer has control over you. Remind yourself that you cried your last tears yesterday.

It's Hard to Say Goodbye

As difficult as it is to say goodbye to a loved one, dear friend, a relationship, or business; there comes a time that you must face the reality that they are no longer a part of your life. I've had to say good-bye countless times to people and things that I held dear to my heart. Was it a painful experience? Yes, it was. But I had to do the inevitable of letting go if I was going to put my life in forward gear.

I would be remiss if I did not tell you that though the people and things were no longer visible in my life, they were still in my thoughts. I still held on to the memories of what used to be, what could have been and more. Satan often uses this method to entangle and ensnare us so that we will not continue to progress. He paralyzes us with our memory.

Satan loves to keep you in a STUCK mode by using the memories of your past. He knows this weakens your effectiveness to do all that God has entrusted into your hands to do. Until you release the thoughts and the memories of yesterday and start living in the NOW, your life will remain stagnant.

He uses this tactic to throw your life in neutral, where you can't move backward or forward, causing your life to come to a standstill. This is just as crippling and debilitating as living in the past. God does not want you standing still. He wants you to continue moving ahead in your kingdom agenda.

When you refuse to release what was once a part of your life but continue to carry it with you, you are allowing it to still have a major affect on your heart. It's not only time to say goodbye to the past, but it's time to totally let go. Confessing it with your mouth only releases it verbally, but your actions releases it mentally and emotionally. As difficult as it may be and as severe the pain you may be feeling at this moment, it's time to let go and move forward so that your life can be healed and restored.

The Grief Process

As I have repeatedly mentioned; when your life suffers a loss or someone leaves your life for whatever reason; there is a sense of loss that is felt. Psychology calls this grief. When we try to prevent this process from taking place, we interfere with the healing process.

Grief is not a negative emotion as it has been made out to be. Matter of fact, grief is very healthy. The reason many are sick today is because of not understanding the power of grief as it relates to the recovery process. Neglecting to grieve properly can be detrimental to your health and prolong the recovery process.

Here's a formula for grief that I put together to help in your transition process, this formula will assist you in getting over your loss, and also give you the strength to rise back up. Try practicing this on a daily basis until you begin to see positive results and your life beginning to re-flourish.

- Gain control of your emotions.
- Refuse to allow the loss to dominate your life.
- Interact with those around you.
- E ngage in the Word of God on a daily basis.
- Forgive, free yourself and move forward.

When David was dealing with the illness of his son, he grieved and mourned and would not eat for days. When Nehemiah received the word that his city had burned down, he also went through a period of grief before he made his request before the King. After David and Nehemiah had come through their grief process; and accepted their loss; they picked themselves back up and went about their daily activities.

Once you have allowed yourself to come through the grieving process, your life will begin to heal again. The ability to exhale will become possible. The spirit of resilience will rise in you once more, and your life will take on new meaning, which will be that of excitement and vitality.

"When I heard these things I sat down abruptly, crying and mourning for several days. I continued fasting and praying before the God of heaven" (Neh. 1:4).

Chapter Seven

MAKING IT ON BROKEN PIECES

Encountering Your Storms

While traveling to Italy, some crewmen were met with a tumultuous storm. This storm beat vehemently upon the ship while a forecast of their future flashed before their eyes. They had no idea whether they would live or die. The spirit of fear and uncertainty had taken hold of the crew, and therefore, caused them to be overtaken with despair. The storm that you are encountering right now has brought on such uncertainty that you don't know if you will survive?

The crewmen knew that if they were to survive the storm, divine intervention was needed. It just so happened, that Apostle Paul was also aboard the ship when the storm arose. Therefore, not only were the crew's lives at stake, but Paul's life was also hanging in the balance. Paul had to make a conscious decision in regards to what to do in this critical juncture if he and the rest of the crew were going to survive the storm.

Paul remained calm even though the rest of the ship was panicking and losing hope. He did what was necessary in a critical situation such as he was facing. The worst thing to do in a crisis is to become overwhelmed with your surroundings to the point that you respond improperly to the emergency at hand. Your very life depends on how you act or react in a dire situation. When we do not allow ourselves to become consumed with the commotion around us, it allows God to speak and show us what to do.

Learn to shut out everything around you, and let God speak to you during your storm. Your future is predicated on you hearing the voice of God. He wants to speak to you and give you a *Rhema* word while you are in the midst of your storm. Open your mind and your spirit to listen to him, and I assure you he will speak to you, and show you your expected end. Instead of reacting to the storm, Paul prayed and God revealed to him that there would be no loss of life aboard the ship. This was the consolation he took to a hopeless crew that desperately needed some optimism.

God Has Given You A Way of Escape

Before the storm arose, God, in his omniscience, knew that a storm would arise, and there would be non-swimmers aboard the ship and that the ship would suffer damage. So, He prepared a way of escape by giving them a survival kit to help them make it through; this survival kit was the residue from the ship. God has also prepared a safety plan for you. Therefore, you can make it through your night, no matter how dark it may be right now, no matter how tempestuous the storm may be raging at this very moment. You will not die in your storm. The storms of life around you will not overtake you but you *can,* you *will,* and you *shall* survive! Because the people listened to Paul and the Centurion; no one lost their lives, instead they all came out with the same testimony; they survived!

Hold on to the Residue

The Centurion commanded the prisoners and those who could swim to jump overboard first and swim to safety. But for those that were non-swimmers, he instructed them to take the planks and the pieces of the ship that was left from the wreckage and swim to dry land. In this way, all were sure to be brought to safety.

The broken pieces that were left from the storm were given to the weak and non-swimmers to hold onto for preservation. These broken pieces would usher them away from danger to safety.

You have to take hold of the broken pieces in your life, and allow them to usher you into the next phase of your destiny. Whatever God did for you before you entered your storm, the testimonies, the victories and the things he allowed you to overcome; grab a hold of those things and allow them to sustain you till the storm blows over.

This Too Will Pass!

When there is nothing left in your life but God, you have enough to start over again. Despite how you feel right now, what you are facing will not last forever; but has an expiration date. This too will pass! There is life after the storm, and behind every dark cloud, there is a ray of sunshine. You will outlast the storm if you keep your eyes on the Master of the Sea. God is in control, and he will speak peace to your situation. Just know that while the storms of life are blowing, you can rest and feel secure in the arms of Jesus while riding through the storm.

Sometimes, storms will take you by surprise, and the unexpected and the seemingly impossible will happen to you. You will find yourself having to hold on, and depend on the very things that seem insignificant to help you keep your head above the water and stay alive. These things are called ***broken pieces***. They are the residue that is left after the storm has blown over. God will use the broken pieces to sustain you in your storm.

You may have suffered major losses as result of the storms that have come into your life. You never envisioned that life would look like this. But, despite your losses: home, finances, family, relationships, you still have what you need to survive on the broken pieces.

"For thou wilt not leave my soul in hell; neither wilt thou suffer thine Holy One to see corruption" (Psalms 16:10).

"Now the soldiers' plan was to kill the prisoners so that none of them would escape by swimming away. But the centurion, wanting to save Paul's life, prevented them from carrying out their plan. He ordered those who could swim to jump overboard first and get to land and the rest were to follow, some on planks and some on pieces of the ship. And in this way all were brought safely to land" (Acts: 27: 42-44).

Predestined to Survive!

While you are in the midst of your most horrific storm, know that no matter how grim the storm looks, if God has given you a word that you will survive, you can be confident in this very promise. The storm could not take Paul under because God had already predestined Paul to stand before Caesar. Therefore, it didn't matter how much the storm raged or how great the magnitude of damage the ship accrued; Paul's life would be spared.

It doesn't matter what you may be facing right now, if God has a predestined place for you to appear, or for you to fulfill a particular assignment; God's word will never return unto him void, but it will accomplish that which he has sent it and also fulfill its purpose. Therefore; the storm must and will come under subjection to God's purpose and plan for your life. You must not allow unbelief and what you are seeing and experiencing at present to cause you to give up and lose hope. It may seem like you are drowning in the sea of life, but know that the Master of the Sea has the wind and the waves in control. God is there on board with you.

People are watching you to see if you are able to handle the adversity, rejection, lies and etc. The enemy does not want you to survive; but I prophesy to you, that you will not die in your storm, but live to declare the works of the Lord. For the hand of God is upon your life and he is going to allow the storm to usher you into your destiny. You will live to tell your story! God has someone on the other side waiting to hear how you survived your storm. You will survive, even if you have to survive on BROKEN PIECES!

"So shall my word be that goeth forth out of my mouth: it shall not return unto me void, but it shall accomplish that which I please, and it shall prosper in the thing whereto I sent it" (Isaiah 55:11).

The Spirit of Resilience

ABOUT THE AUTHOR

Author, teacher and minister, Dr. Newton is a sought-out transformational coach and empowerment specialist. She has earned the reputation as a motivator and a midwife for spiritual birthing. Dr. Newton combines her wealth of leadership, expertise, spiritual enlightenment along with her passion for souls to aide her in releasing messages that encourage, empower, and transform.

Dr. Newton is the Founder and CEO of the LADY Institute; a Personal Training and Development center that is responsible for helping women *"grow from the inside out."* She facilitates workshops that focus on self-esteem, goal setting, and personal development. She is also the Founder/CEO of BN Enterprises and The Winner's Circle, a social network that has been designed to assist women in achieving personal growth through coaching, training, and cutting-edge resources.

Dr. Newton is the author of several books entitled, "When Destiny Calls, The Life of a Dreamer, The Spirit of Resilience, In Pursuit of Destiny and many more." They are a must read for those who are serious about fulfilling their Destiny and carrying out the assignment upon their lives.

Dr. Newton is a graduate of Jacksonville Theological Seminary where she received her bachelor's degree in Biblical studies. She is also a graduate of John Wesley University, where she received her bachelor's degree in Christian Counseling. She obtained her Master of Divinity from Christian Leadership University and her Doctorate from Covenant Theological Seminary.

Dr. Newton continually sows the seed for personal growth, offering hope, and a new direction toward positive self-image. Countless men and women have been transformed by the wisdom and anointing that rest upon her life. In addition to preaching across the country, she hosts and presents seminars, workshops, and conferences. Her life has touched thousands as she travels around the nation proclaiming the gospel message. She is a well sought-out speaker for this 21st century because of her uncanny ability to inspire, motivate, and transform the lives of those who follow her.

Made in the USA
Columbia, SC
15 August 2019